FOR WHAT WE ARE ABOUT TO RECEIVE

Thirty Everyday Stories

Violet Neumann

with Teresa Klassen

Produced by:

FriesenPress
Suite 300 – 852 Fort Street
Victoria, BC, Canada V8W 1H8

www.friesenpress.com

Distributed to the trade by The Ingram Book Company

To my children, grandchildren, and the generations to come:

I love the LORD because He hears my voice
and my prayer for mercy.
Because He bends down to listen,
I will pray as long as I have breath!

Psalm 116:1-2

TABLE OF CONTENTS

SCRIPTURE

The Scripture passages used in this book were written on the inside cover of Violet's Bible. They were verses that were meaningful to her along the way.

MANY THANKS TO...

Linnea Archondous, Melanie Friesen, Sherry Jackson and Shauna Thornton for your assistance in typing this manuscript. There were many more offers to help than pages to type; thanks to everyone for your kindness.

Thank you to Michael Klassen for letting us use your journal entry as a framework for "Living Well/Dying Well."

Thank you to Joris Kempers, Ellen Kempers and Heidi Kaethler for assisting with the editing process.

About The Title

"For what we are about to receive
We give thanks."

– A Traditional Prayer of Thankfulness

You will find, as you read, that Violet received so much from the hand of God. Some things were amazingly good right from the start. Other situations were challenging and didn't seem at all good at the time.

There were many things she didn't want to receive!

Still, God was proven faithful over and over and so she came to decide that, no matter what, she would give thanks.

No one knows what is around the corner, will it be pleasant or will it be hard? But when we place our trust in the Lord Jesus, knowing that His plans are not to harm us, but to bring about good, we can always say, "For what we are about to receive, we give thanks."

INTRODUCTION

I have always been a list person, and at some point in the 1960's I began to keep a list of the things I noticed God doing in my life. They were short entries like:

- ☐ Surgery after Lloyd was born (angel)
- ☐ The dirt pile (no rain)
- ☐ Moving from Vancouver to Richmond (unfinished house)
- ☐ Harold's heart attack.

It wouldn't have made sense to anyone else, but those few words were enough to remind me of specific stories where I had seen God at work in my life.

I kept adding to the list and in 1989 I began to write out each story in more detail. I have no idea why 1989 was the year. Maybe I should have written that on my list too! In any case, that was the year. I wrote these stories for my own good to "count my blessings," so to speak.

As I wrote, I kept my children, Lloyd and Teresa, in mind. I wanted them to see that even in my own simple stories that truly the Lord is God. I took to heart Psalm 71: 17-18,

Since my youth, O God, you have taught me, and to this day
I declare your marvelous deeds.
Even when I am old and grey, do not forsake me,
O God, till I declare your power to the next generation,
your might to all who are to come.

I never imagined that these stories would be of interest to anyone else but when I found (at age 75) that I had stage-four pancreatic cancer, I told Teresa about my book of stories. It was more of a comment in passing: "By the way, I have this book of stories..." She was the one to suggest a story-time each night and one thing led to another.

I lived with my daughter Teresa, son-in-law Michael, and their children and whoever was home at 10 pm would come downstairs and listen to me read one of my stories. Other people joined in like my brothers and sisters and friends of Michael and Teresa's family; it became a beautiful, quiet time of reflection with laughter and tears and questions and at the end, prayer.

Then Teresa said, "I think we need to make a book of these to share with others, mom." I had no idea it would all become this! So here I am at 75 with my time on earth dwindling, never imagining myself a writer, never thinking these stories would mean much to anyone else, putting together a book!

These are not all of my stories, of course. The apostle John said in John 21:25,

Jesus did many other things as well.
If every one of them were written down,
I suppose that even the whole world would not have room
for the books that would be written.

I feel the same! These are not all of the things I have experienced; just a representation

I hope, with my simple words, that these stories testify to the power of Jesus Christ and my great love for Him and I hope that whoever reads this will feel compelled to seek Him also with heart, mind and soul.

Violet Neumann
February 2013

About Violet

By Teresa Klassen

My mother, Violet was born in Steinbach, Manitoba on December 30, 1937 to Peter and Marie Kaethler. They were two people who loved Jesus and brought their family up to know and love the Lord. She was their sixth child, with two older brothers, one younger, and three older sisters.

In Steinbach, the family lived on a bit of acreage with an old barn and a very small house. It had no glass in the windows at first, no electricity and no running water. They had a fuel oil lamp to read by and a wood burning stove to cook with and to heat the house, as well as a wooden plank floor, a water well with a pump, and an outhouse not too far away. The bath water was heated on the stove and emptied into a round, metal tub. All the kids took turns in that water, from oldest to youngest, which mom never found quite fair.

The family was poor but so were most families back then during the Great Depression so it didn't seem very unusual. If the farming didn't bring in enough, mom's father would go help other farmers with their harvesting to make an extra bit of money. As poor as they were, mom remembered feeling quite carefree in those years and unaware of the struggles her parents were having to stay afloat. They had no neighbors for miles and so her friends were her brothers and sisters, and what a great time they had!

When mom was five the family moved to British Columbia nearby the little community of Yarrow, which is near the city of Chilliwack. My mom and her mother had gone on a pre-trip to scout out the land which mom remembered very well. They went by train and arrived in Yarrow to meet a whole host of relatives. Mom was very petite for her age and had thick blonde hair. She was a tomboy as well and was not used to being passed around from relative to relative as she was always being patted on the head and kissed and held. They always said mom was shy, which she hated!

The men had prickly beards and smelled like the barn and the women were, as mom wrote, of a size that had indicated they had borne many children. To have seven to ten children was not uncommon. Their laps were short and she wasn't sure what to hang on to so that she wouldn't slide off. It sure is funny what a person remembers.

The family did eventually move to Yarrow. At first they rented a place, and then they bought a farm on Vedder Mountain. It had a great view and 60 acres of land. Mom wrote down many of her memories from their life on the mountain. She remembers the large garden they had, feeding the chickens and collecting their eggs, the tractor they drove, and the butchering parties when they made sausage, roasts, ground beef and bacon.

Mom loved working with her father on the farm. Many of her chores were with her father as she was not much of an indoor person. She had a wonderful relationship with him and would often say that he was the greatest influence in her life. She saw how her father enjoyed life in good and bad times, his compassion for other people and tremendous faith in God. When they experienced hardships or illnesses she always felt secure because God was very real to her dad and she trusted what he said. He would often say that things always would work out for good if they trusted God.

Whenever possible mom's family went to Sunday school and church. The custom in those days was men on one side and women and children on the other. The adults were very strict about children being seen and not heard and mom was always terrified that she would get a tap on the shoulder for being noisy.

At home her parents talked freely about God; Bible reading and prayer in their home was carried on regularly basis morning and evening. Mom says that she was keenly aware of the fact that she was a sinner and so at the age of ten she asked Jesus to forgive her and to lead her life. She was excited about this important thing she had done. She knew she had made an important decision, and that something had happened between her and God that would change the rest of her life. At 18 she was water baptized.

In 1956 mom was in her grade 12 year when the family moved to Vancouver. Mom never graduated from high school as she needed to work when they got there. In Vancouver she found a job with a Medical Insurance company and worked for them for many years. At that time she gave ninety percent of her income to her parents to help them and in order to afford clothing and bus fare mom did day-work on Saturdays. She says she never regretted giving her money to her parents because it helped them get into a house and she was glad she could do it.

At that time Mom was attending Fraserview Mennonite Brethren Church and it was there that mom met my dad, Harold Neumann. The family was pretty involved in making sure a young lady would have a suitable match and so questions like "did he come from a good church-going family, was he educated, did anyone know his relatives?" were some of the things that mattered.

Mom's parents knew dad's parents well enough to know they were a Christian family, serving as deacons and elders in the church and his father was a lay minister. Dad himself was educated, just completing his engineering degree. They dated for a year and then were married in March 1959.

So much of my mom's story from this point to the end is affected by my dad's story as dad was a complicated person. He presented himself one way to mom when they were dating but when they were married, as mom describes it, three weeks in she saw a very different side to him. He was not the person she thought he was. What a discouraging realization that was for her, but Mom had made a commitment to him and felt convicted that she needed to stick with that. She called out to God and would call out to God again and again over the years for His help and guidance in her marriage and in raising their family. She knew, even though she was married, that in many things she would be on her own.

In 1964 my brother Lloyd was born and in 1968 I was born. After each of us, mom required a major surgery and we were put in the care of relatives. Facing illness really caused her to get on her knees and look for answers from God. She realized she had known God all her life but she questioned at this point how well she knew Him. Did she really have confidence in God? Did she really trust Him?

She vowed if she came through this surgery and recovered that she would devote the rest of her life to really knowing God, loving Him, and serving Him. God became very real to mom along the way, which gave her strength to handle the many difficulties she would face. Instead of wearing her down, mom's troubles made her a grateful person. As I wrote this, I thought, have I ever really heard my mom complain about her circumstances? Not that I can remember!

Who knew that the girl that everyone said was shy was actually made of iron? She had to have been. How is it that I had such a happy childhood when there were so many things going wrong in our life? My mom put on such a brave face and worked so hard to make sure my life and Lloyd's life was filled with opportunity and joy. We weren't even aware of the burdens mom was carrying.

Mom was so selfless in these things and as I look at my own life and my own reactions, I am so challenged by how she handled it all. Her source of strength is clear if you read her stories. Not by might, not by power but by God's Spirit she became this conqueror.

It is hard to put seventy-five years of experiences onto paper. Actually, it's quite impossible! Life is more than facts and places and where mom lived, and the events she lived through. Mom's story is so much about her walk with God and the lessons she learned, the incredible answers to her prayers and spiritual struggles.

In one of mom's notebooks she wrote, "If I were a writer, perhaps I could convey to you the depth and feelings of what is really in me and the extreme gratitude I feel to God for carrying me all these years." The funny thing is mom was a writer, and she wrote pages and pages and pages about answers to prayer.

For the past fifteen years mom lived with my husband and family in West Kelowna. What a blessing mom was to us! I can't adequately describe it. What a lot of joy we had living together! Mom enriched our lives and along the way she had a second life as a widow that was so different from the first part. She discovered new things about herself, she became a significant part of our church family and so well-loved.

She found and used her gifts, and discovered more gifts that she ever thought she had. She allowed herself to be stretched and she lived sacrificially and courageously in so many ways. What great laughs we had, wonderful vacations together, countless meals, and a million conversations.

In January 2013 she found out she had pancreatic cancer.

It was during this time that she casually mentioned her "book of stories." As I paged through them, I thought it would be wonderful to hear her tell them so as a family we began to meet with mom at ten in the evening each night to listen to these stories of faith. It was redemptive and holy and right. Mom was not at all afraid of dying and she wasn't depressed or discouraged but was lovely, faith-filled and strong.

Mom wrote, "I have done things and experienced things I never dreamed I would. Nor had I dreamed about all the places I would see. I don't know what the path or road He will lead me to next, but then life is an adventure with God leading the way to the most unexpected places."

Early on mom vowed to God that she would commit her life to getting to know Him. She has so many simple yet powerful stories that have come from fulfilling this promise to God, and many of those stories are found in this book; thirty of them!

FAMILY

**Peter Kaethler (my father) married
Marie Harder (my mother).**

They had seven children:

Hildegarde
Anne
Jake
Peter
Erika
Violet *(that's me)*
John.

I married Harold Neumann.

We had two children:

Lloyd
Teresa.

Lloyd married Roberta Loewen.

They had one child:

Levi.

Teresa married Michael Klassen.

They had four children:

Alecia
Mikaela
Joshua
Nathan.

1. A Visitor

* * *

July 23, 1964 was a day I will never forget as it was a day of extremes: extreme pain and extreme joy! It was a day long waited for. I had walked through a wonderful pregnancy. I wasn't sick a day and now our first child was born. Our son, Lloyd, was a beautiful baby, but because of the difficult birth he was placed in an incubator for a few days to make sure he would be okay. We recovered very well and soon went home.

I dedicated Lloyd to the Lord and I prayed over him. My heart overflowed with joy over this new life God had given us to enjoy and be responsible for. He was a very good baby and so at two months, my husband Harold, his parents, little Lloyd and I took a three-week holiday to North Dakota to visit Harold's sister and her family. Everything went very well until we were on our way home. I started to feel sick and after we were home for a few days I became extremely ill.

Immediately tests began. It became a long process of waiting. I had to wait for x-rays and all kinds of test results. I learned that I had a serious problem with a valve that was attached to my kidney and I would need major surgery. That too required several months of waiting before something opened up for me.

The waiting gave me time to think. This type of surgery was very new and if it wasn't successful I would lose my kidneys before long. I had confidence in the doctor but for the first time in my life I was really afraid of eternity. What if I died? Was I really ready to meet my Creator?

I knew I had made a decision at age ten when I asked Jesus to come and lead my life and I knew if I sinned and asked for forgiveness I was forgiven. I had read the Bible and I knew a lot about God. I had attended church all my life but I didn't know God as a friend. I knew facts about Him, but I hadn't experienced His care. I hadn't tested my faith or relied on God to do the impossible, and I didn't know if I could trust that His promises were true.

In my desperation I thumbed through the Bible trying to find some verses to comfort and encourage me. I found Philippians 4: 4-8 and memorized them:

> *Rejoice in the Lord always. I will say it again: Rejoice!*
> *Let your gentleness be evident to all. The Lord is near.*

*Do not be anxious about anything, but in every situation,
by prayer and petition, with thanksgiving, present your requests to
God.
And the peace of God, which transcends all understanding,
will guard your hearts and your minds in Christ Jesus.
Finally, brothers and sisters, whatever is true, whatever is noble,
whatever is right, whatever is pure, whatever is lovely,
whatever is admirable—if anything is excellent or praiseworthy—
think about such things.*

I asked God to draw near to me and show me the meaning of those verses. I desperately wanted more than what I was experiencing in my life and in my relationship with God. I promised that if God brought me through this that I would dedicate the rest of my life to really knowing Him. Day after day I talked to God and by the time I entered the hospital I had worked through my fears and I had found peace.

My sister Hildegarde and her family agreed to take care of little Lloyd for the three months I would need for recovery time. I knew he would receive the best of care with the sister who had loved me so well all my life. I knew I would be spending a lot of time in the hospital and resigned myself to it. I had no idea beyond that what to expect.

I had a private room at the Vancouver General Hospital and when I entered the nurse told me to undress, slip on the hospital clothes and sit on the chair near the window and wait for further instructions. I did so and waited. Waiting is not a bad thing; I found it allows a person to collect their thoughts and in the quiet listen for the whisper of God.

It didn't take long and a man dressed in white scrubs came in and stood in front of the built-in dresser, which was across from where I was sitting. He was of medium build with reddish blonde hair, which was short and clean-cut. He had a well put-together look about him.

He asked me how I was feeling and if I was afraid. I said I had confidence in the doctor, but it didn't feel very good to be alone away from my family. He said he would drop in quite a few times to see me and asked if I would like him to walk beside me when I would be wheeled into surgery. I said that would be really nice and he left.

He did what he said he would do. He dropped by before my surgery and he was with me when I was wheeled in to surgery and then he stopped in several times a day after the surgery. There was something very comforting about that.

I was extremely sick after surgery. At one point the nurse sent an alarm and I was bombarded with doctors and nurses to see if I was bleeding internally. They kept a close eye on me and through all of this, the man in white continued to visit. He never touched me or asked medical questions and in fact he usually just asked, "How are you?" He always stood by the dresser for some time, quietly, and then after awhile he would leave.

I thought it was so kind of him to visit as it always gave me a real sense of peace and of being cared for when he was there. Except for the time when I was wheeled to surgery he always came alone and left alone. At one point I was curious about him and I asked him what his job was and he replied that a part of his job was to see that I was happy. I was satisfied with that answer at the time.

On the third day after surgery I was extremely sick, the pain was almost unbearable and I cried almost all day. He came in to see me several times that day saying nothing and standing at a distance. Later on in that night I felt like I was floating and my heart was slowing down to the point where I didn't have any energy to press the alarm and I didn't care. All at once he came and stood right beside my bed and his presence was deeply comforting. I didn't say anything and neither did he and after awhile I fell asleep.

The next morning very early before the nurse came in and he came in again and stood in his usual place by the dresser. He asked me how I was feeling and I said I felt like the worst was over. I said, "last night I felt like I wasn't going to make it." His reply startled me. He said, "I know. But I'm glad you made it," and he left.

The nurse came by later and I thought I would ask her about him. I told her about this medical person who kept coming by and how comforting his presence had been to me. She looked at me with a puzzled look. She said there was no male nurse, doctor or other staff on that floor or the floor above or below that fit his description. She said that none of the staff would have that kind of time to spend with one patient. She had worked on that ward for many years, had been there the entire time I had been in the hospital, and knew all the staff very well and what was going on. She said there simply wasn't anyone there by that description.

She left and now I was puzzled until I realized something. It occurred to me that my visitor must have been an angel. I couldn't think of any other explanation:

- I was under no medication when he first began to visit so I wasn't imagining that he was there.
- He didn't act like a medical person. He asked no medical question. He never once touched me.

- He dressed like a medical person and if he hadn't I would have been leery of him.

- He didn't return once I was feeling better and I started to question his presence, probably because his job there was done as far as his visible presence was concerned.

- I had a sense of peace and contentment when he was there that I really could not explain.

I went through the remainder of the healing process knowing that something amazing had happened. Not only was I learning to trust God in a new way but also God had given me an experience, and a gift I would never forget.

God's Word became a living thing in my life from then on.

- I received a deep and absolute conviction that God was real.

- I knew that God loved me.

- I knew that He had a plan for me.

- I knew I had a guardian angel as the Bible says we do.

- I received total healing from that surgery.

- I knew I could tell God everything and rejoice in Him in all circumstances.

I didn't tell anyone about what had happened at the time. Somehow the time didn't seem right before that and I kept this story close to my heart. However the experience changed me and I began to read the Bible and pray on a more consistent basis. I asked God to work in me and help me grow as a person and as a Christian.

When I finally did talk about this experience I chose to do so one time with our Bible study group and another time with mother and sisters at a luncheon. It inspired a very special time of sharing and praising God. I felt the time was right because God was glorified through it.

I never expected that God would meet me the way He did. I am still amazed at how He took care of me in such a personal way and this was really the beginning of truly understanding how God can lift our burdens and give us peace. I began to see how God does things that are beyond our understanding. It made me so thankful and taught me to give thanks in the future, no matter how difficult the circumstances.

I received God's healing touch and His comfort and presence. For extending the days of my life and for what I learned through this I give thanks.

2. The Potatoes

"What do you mean, 'If I can'?" Jesus asked.
"Anything is possible if a person believes."

Mark 9:23

* * *

When we lived in Richmond, the Mennonite Central Committee of Canada and the U.S. had a week of meetings in our church *(MCC is an organization that works all over the world, helping the poor)*. I was asked to help with serving the food for the final celebration meal and a wonderful capable woman named Nettie was in charge. As always she was well organized and prepared, leading her team to always have the food hot, ready and served on time. She was always prepared for extra people and had set up for that already.

When the time came to serve the food we discovered that the scalloped potatoes were far from done. She had prepared this type of a meal many, many times and this had never happened before. We didn't know what to do! The room was full of people already, anticipating a great meal. We asked the pastor if the meal could wait another twenty more minutes and he said that would be fine but it couldn't be later because quite a few people needed to drive or fly home. As we looked at the crowd coming in we could see that many more people had shown up than expected and even more tables were being set up! We were sure that we were going to run short of food. It felt like the meal was going to be a disaster!

After the twenty minutes were up we all sampled the potatoes and agreed that they could not be served the way they were, as the potatoes were crunchy, the sauce hadn't thickened and they were simply not done! Nettie was quiet a moment and then announced we needed a modern day miracle! She asked us to form a circle. There were around ten people in that circle including Nettie. She said we should all say whether we believed a miracle could happen and could God do something for us? She said if we believed He could we needed to have a verse of Scripture to back it up and then take one pan out of the oven and serve the first scoop as an indication of faith that they would be done.

No one wanted to commit to that and I wrestled inwardly over her request. I was learning to trust God but wasn't sure if I was ready to step out with that kind of faith! At the same time I wanted to believe in that miracle. I felt if I said no then wasn't I in some way denying my faith in God?

I said I needed a couple of minutes because I couldn't think of a verse. I was nervous and nothing was coming to mind. When I couldn't think of a verse and with my heart beating fast I decided to move towards the oven anyway. When I did the verse came to me! I said out loud, *"If you can believe, all things are possible to him who believes"* (this is found in Mark 9:23).

We took out a large pan of steaming potatoes and I was handed a metal serving spoon. I served the first portion of potatoes not really knowing what would happen.

- ☐ The potatoes were totally done and tasted very good.
- ☐ The sauce had thickened and the potatoes were tender.
- ☐ People who generally didn't like scalloped potatoes commented on how good they were and asked for seconds!
- ☐ There were enough potatoes for everyone plus the helpers.

Not only did God do a miracle cooking those raw potatoes but He also added His special touch so that they tasted exceptionally good, and multiplied them so that there were enough for everyone.

Later on when the kitchen helpers were talking about the miracle it became clear to me that I had benefited in a special way. The step of faith I had taken had once again increased my confidence in God and shown me that His promises are true.

I learned that God often comes through only when I am willing to make a move of faith. This story gave me confidence for so many other situations I would face and I learned that though others might only ask for things that were "doable" I could ask the impossible of God.

For this miracle we received and for the lesson I learned I give thanks.

3. The Landscaping

"But if you remain in me and my words remain in you, you may ask for anything you want, and it will be granted!"

John 15:7

* * *

What am I capable of? Over the years of my life I have found on my own I can do little, but with Jesus, little is enough. He can take my ordinary life, with my limited skills, my small amount of knowledge, and do something powerful with it. He can use me in my weakness to accomplish His purposes.

When we relocated to Surrey we moved into a new house with no landscaping. It really needed to be done but had been on hold for quite some time as my husband Harold couldn't help due to health issues related to his heart. My son Lloyd *(a teenager then)* was recovering from leg surgery and couldn't help either. My daughter Teresa was attending a school that was over an hour away and had very long days. Friends and family had busy lives of their own. No, if the yard was going to be done, I would have to do it.

After I had made some plans for the yard, I prayed about them and when I felt the time was right I proceeded. Somehow God would give me the strength I needed and in faith,

- ☐ I ordered a huge truck-load of top soil delivered.
- ☐ I organized the tools to wheel and shovel it into place.
- ☐ I arranged for the sod to be sent the day after the topsoil was delivered.

There was no turning back now!

First thing in the morning I rolled up my sleeves, got my shovel and went out-doors to tackle it but no sooner had I begun to shovel the topsoil it began to rain. When it rains in the Vancouver/Surrey area, it really rains! The little bit of rain became a downpour and the more I worked the more tired I became. As I looked at the rain soaking into the dirt I realized the soil was going to become heavier and heavier. I had no plastic to cover the soil and we were in a new neighborhood with few neighbors and I didn't know who to call on to help me.

I went inside and sat down. I had not factored in the weather on my list of things to be concerned about. This could all end up being a disaster. So I brought the matter to God. I prayed about it, thought for a few moments, sensing what God would have me do and a plan came to mind. Here was a chance to show my children how God will look after us if we call on Him.

I said to Lloyd, "I am going out there to shovel and wheel. I have asked God to stop the rain from hitting the front yard and also to give me the strength to finish the job today." I then quoted Philippians 4:13: "I can do all things through Christ who strengthens me." I am not sure what he thought of that!

Here is what happened that afternoon...... no rain fell on the front yard!!! It rained on our neighbor's yard, it rained in the back yard but my front yard was completely dry. I did not grow tired at all! I had worked steady from 9:00 a.m. to 12:00 noon. I then took a break and worked from 1:30 in the afternoon to 5:00 in the evening. At 5:00 I had finished placing the soil and raking it so that it was ready for the sod and I had energy to spare!

In the evening I was not tired. Harold and I went to Bible study and after that we walked for three miles in our subdivision. I shared my experiences with Harold as we walked, and in our Bible study group and to our children..... God is good!

God saw my need and helped me. I am not sure what He thought about my prayer but I saw that He cared for me and was willing to help me in the most practical way. I had no sore muscles or pain as a result of the work and in fact I felt terrific! I can't explain it any other way than to say that God worked more than I did!

I have prayed prayers that some might think were ridiculous, and God has smiled and answered them and for this I give thanks.

4. FROM HOUSE TO HOUSE

"Keep on asking, and you will receive what you ask for. Keep on seeking,
and you will find. Keep on knocking, and the door will be opened to you."

Matthew 7:7

* * *

What can we bring to God in prayer? Everything!!!!!! I have
learned, along the way, how He delights in hearing the voices
of His children and loves it when we seek Him on all matters. I
could tell so many stories of how God has opened doors for me
and sometimes very literally when it came to the homes I have
lived in.

Part one

When we lived in Vancouver, our son Lloyd was a very active
four-year old and our daughter Teresa was a baby. The area of the

city where we lived was not a great place to raise children. The back lane was a problem as it was near a busy intersection and the yard was quite sloped which made playing challenging for young children. Also, the neighborhood children across the lane were not kind to Lloyd and threw rocks at him and no matter what I said or did they would not stop. I became convinced that we needed to move to another house with a yard where the children could play safely.

I began to pray earnestly but privately about what to do as I wanted to be careful and wise about it.

It didn't take long and my sister-in-law, Helen who lived in Richmond, phoned and said there was a house across the street that had just come up for sale. She had thought of me even though I had not told anyone about my prayer. The phone call came right out of the blue! We went and looked at it, bought it, and moved in shortly after! The house needed some work, but it had a huge yard, big enough to subdivide so that we could add another house at a later date.

Four years later we began building a second house on the property with the intention of selling our present home and moving into the new one. I wasn't sure how it would all work out as the real estate market was weak at the time. I just committed it all to the Lord.

Before the construction of the new house was finished and before the house we were living in was put up for sale, there was a knock on the door and a man asked how much we were asking for our house and how quickly could we move. That was quite funny to me because we hadn't even worked out those details yet or put up a sign! God was at work!

We agreed to sell much sooner than we had thought we would and moved out into our new and unfinished house. I had no kitchen, no finished flooring and our bathtub was our only supply of water! But I didn't mind as I loved how God was looking after us and had gone ahead of us to make arrangements. We didn't have to try and sell through a realtor and that saved us a lot of money and extra concern.

We lived in the new house like we were camping, and this provided for some great memories for the children!

Part two

Now back to the house in Vancouver because there is more to that story. The Vancouver house just was not selling and Harold and I could not afford two mortgages! I kept praying about it as it seemed so clear that God had led us to move to Richmond so why didn't we see any movement on the house?

One day a couple came by and told us they loved the Vancouver house but the problem was they were short on a down payment and they really wanted the house though! They asked if we would consider selling it on what is called an "Agreement For Sale," which meant they would pay for the home in installments. After I had prayed about it and Harold and I had discussed it, we said yes. They faithfully made monthly payments to us for a long time.

Sometimes, in the moment, you don't know exactly why things happen the way they do and it is not like we always figure it out, but in this case, I did. Why our house didn't sell in the conventional way and why we allowed this couple to make payments to us year after year all made sense years later .....seventeen years later to be exact.

Harold needed a new vehicle to get to work and back but I was very concerned that we would not go into debt over it. Harold didn't really see any other way than taking out a loan and so I began to pray. I prayed earnestly and specifically that the money the couple still owed us on that Vancouver house could be paid out to us out by a certain Monday evening, and before Harold could secure a loan.

That Monday evening the man who we had an agreement with on the Vancouver house phoned and said he was changing jobs and the requirement was that he have no debt. He asked if he could pay us out with a small discount? We agreed. He had never missed a payment in seventeen years. That amount of money got us the truck and kept us out of debt!

I love the way God works things out when we rely on Him and aren't impatient. Over and over I learned that God knows what our needs will be long before we do. He is creative with how He accomplishes His purposes and I think He delights in surprising us! I found that going to Him first saved me so much grief later!

When I have prayed I have opened up my hands for God to give me what He thinks is best in the way He thinks is best. For what I have received, time and time again, I give thanks.

5. The Christmas Gift

"The generous will prosper; those who refresh others will
themselves be refreshed."

Proverbs 11:25

* * *

I grew up in a family that experienced a lot of poverty. My parents
were immigrants and came to Canada with next to nothing. They
made a life for themselves but finances were always a struggle.
When I got married we had our lean times too but I never felt
terribly worried that we couldn't provide for ourselves.

Then, while we were living in Richmond, Harold had an accident.
He fell from the roof while fixing something on our chimney and
was confined to a wheelchair for quite a long time. Things were
really rough for us financially as a result. Harold was not able to
run his development/construction business, our bank account

began to dwindle, and the cupboards in my kitchen were looking pretty bare!

Christmas was only a few weeks away and I was really exhausted from all the extra responsibilities placed on my shoulders because of Harold's injury. I didn't feel like doing Christmas baking and shopping was pointless as we couldn't afford to buy gifts or any extras.

Before I had time to pray specifically for groceries or for gifts to give and before I could come to God and ask for encouragement to keep our spirits up, He had it all planned.

Harold was on his feet a little bit more around Christmas and one Sunday he went to church and I didn't as I was just too tired. When he came home he sat down at the kitchen table and the look on his face told me that something had touched him deeply. He handed me an envelope that the pastor had given him. Someone had asked our pastor to pass something on to us and did not want to be identified. In it was a note of encouragement and five one hundred dollar bills.

Five hundred dollars would not solve everything but it was such a beautiful gesture that we both sat and cried out of sheer joy. It was such a special Christmas for our family and we saw with new eyes how it was a time of sharing and caring and a time to encourage others. That day I decided I wanted to be a certain kind of person, the kind of person who listens for God's prompts and then just follows through, to be generous to those I know and to those I don't even know. I have tried to live this way ever since.

Not only did we receive a very specific encouragement but God made it clear to me that this is how I should live my life helping others when they are in need and in whatever form that might be.

For showing me the importance of being sensitive to others hurts and needs and inspiring me to be obedient to promptings, I give thanks.

6. FIRST CAR

"Though good advice lies deep within the heart, a person with
understanding will draw it out."

Proverbs 20:5

* * *

When our son Lloyd was fourteen years old I saw restlessness
in him and it concerned me. The teenage years were setting in
and I felt he needed something to keep him busy and hold his
interest and also give him an opportunity to learn something. I
really felt an urgency around this and prayed for understanding
as I needed an idea for my son and knew that God could give it
to me.

Sure enough, after I talked to God about it the idea came. I
wasn't sure what Harold would think but prayed that he would
be open to what might have seemed like an unusual solution.

I talked to Harold about buying an old "junker" car for Lloyd to work on. Lloyd was so creative and handy and interested in all things mechanical that I thought this would be a fun and time-consuming project for him. I didn't care if the car worked or didn't work and I asked Harold if we could just buy something and let him do whatever he wanted with it.

Harold didn't have a problem with the idea, looked around and found an old, beat-up Valiant for $125.00 and it even came with an additional car motor to take apart. As it turned out the car had been in an accident and only needed a few parts and a paint job and other than that it was in good condition. Lloyd loved "tinkering" on it and got it to the place where it was in decent running condition. Lloyd even took our air-sprayer (for painting houses, not vehicles) and painted his car with a very, very thick coat of brown paint.

With the other motor Lloyd and his friends took it apart and put it together again and it was a great learning experience for them. The garage and his clothes were always a greasy mess and Lloyd constantly had dirt under his nails! But then, what did it matter? I could only see the benefits of the experience and what it could mean in the future for him.

This project turned out to be a very good one all around. Not only did the car fill many hours of Lloyd's day as he managed to fix it up but when he was old enough he ended up driving it for many years. He and his friends would pile into that old Valiant and down the road they would go having a lot of great fun. If that car could talk it would have many a story to tell (perhaps I wouldn't want to hear them all)!

I learned that sometimes an idea comes and even if it doesn't make total and practical sense it is right. I learned to recognize ideas God was giving to me. I am so grateful how God gives wisdom in this way and how He shows us what to do and gives the confidence to go ahead with it knowing He will work out the details. The Bible says in Luke 11:9,

> *Ask and you will receive, seek and you will find,*
> *knock and the door will be opened.*

That verse has become an incredible reality for me many times over.

For seeing how God is so practical, and for learning that He is willing to be very involved with our parenting problems, I give thanks.

7. A FATHER'S LOVE

"A friend is always loyal, and a brother is born to help in time of need."

Proverbs 17:17

* * *

When I was pregnant the second time I was extremely happy and the entire nine months went very well. I stayed on a strict nutritious diet so that I wouldn't gain more than seventeen pounds as the doctor advised. He wanted to make sure my kidneys would be okay through it all. The delivery was difficult but worth it all. God gave me a beautiful, healthy baby girl, Teresa Joy. That name has been an appropriate one!

I enjoyed my children very much and considered myself very fortunate and blessed. In many ways they were so different from one another but I saw their gifts and felt so privileged to be able to encourage both Lloyd and Teresa to use them. I delighted in hearing their childish chatter and listen to their ideas and dreams. Lloyd was a magnificent builder of forts, and go-carts, and motors! All the neighborhood kids would peer through our fence to see what Lloyd was up to. And Teresa was clearly a writer! She had such an imagination and wrote wonderful stories and notes. She was always brimming with ideas and never bored for a minute.

After Teresa was born I dedicated her to the Lord and promised God I would disciple her under His guidance so that she would become a beautiful, giving, woman, pleasing and useful.

Several months later I again became very sick and when the doctors couldn't find the cause of the kidney infections they blamed it on me saying that I was an over-anxious mother! I didn't think I was anxious at all as I just knew something was going wrong with my health!

My brother John felt convinced he should take me to the Mayo Clinic in the United States and he arranged everything and covered all of my expenses *(what a blessing!).* When all the tests were done, the clinic advised me to have surgery as soon as possible or I would lose my kidneys. They said that even with the surgery I probably had only about ten years of kidney function left and then would need to be on a dialysis machine. We went back home with this new information and a couple of months later I had surgery.

One day while still in the hospital my father came to the hospital by himself to see me. He saw how sick I was and knew that my kidney function was not good. My dad was a gentle and quiet man. My mother usually did most of the talking around our home and he let her. On the day my dad came to visit he wanted to know how I was. I will always remember how kindly he looked at me and then in his own quiet way he said that he had been thinking about me and had come to a decision. He didn't want me to argue and he was firm about this, that should I need a kidney he wanted to give me one of his. He had prayed about it, talked it over with my mother and discussed it with his family doctor already.

I was so very moved by his offer and I hardly knew what to say. My father was in his late sixties so how could he possibly donate a kidney? It was such an impractical offer but actually it was more than that. What my father was saying was, "I will lay down my life for yours so you can live."

Is there any greater love then that?

I highly respected my father as a person and as a Christian. For many years he showed a special concern for my family and I. We had worked together so often and as a child on the farm he and I would work together in the barn. Now that I was an adult he would always come and help me plant a garden and he did this year after year! I remember being out there in the fresh air turning the soil and planting the seeds. We would talk about things and he often talked about God and his faith in Him as we worked. He also spoke of how he cared so deeply for others and about their final destiny. Then we would just quietly work side by side. Oh I loved my father and these afternoons working together! He was always willing to come and help with whatever I needed.

In my hospital room that day my father demonstrated such a beautiful and selfless kind of love. I will never forget it. It was beyond any gift I had ever received. He did not end up needing to donate his kidney but I would never forget his love, his tenderness, and the way he was willing to sacrifice his own health for mine.

My father died a few years later, but left me with a wealth of good memories.

Dad, always the outdoorsman, was on a hike on Mount Baker *(in Washington State),* wanting to see the glacier there. He saw the glacier, had lunch and sat down and died. After his death I walked into the garden we had planted together and had a good cry and then I praised God for those good experiences. I thanked God for allowing him to die on Mount Baker in a beautiful setting with a painless, quick death. What a lovely home-going to eternal joy!

My father's love gave me a glimpse of my Heavenly Father's love for me. In turn I have tried to love like that, to love deeply as Christ commands us to. I praise God that He has sent loving people into my life to help me in times of need and so many have given sacrificially.

For being on the receiving end of such great love and compassion, I give thanks.

8. SPECIAL NEEDS KIDS

"But those who do what is right come to the light so others can see that they are doing what God wants."

John 3:21

* * *

When I was working for a private school in Richmond as a secretary I got to know all the children and their families and I became quite aware of people's needs through this experience. One couple I got to know had two children in the school. Their job was running a group home for eight special needs kids. Some of the children were nearly blind and some mentally challenged while others were unruly, destructive and loud. This family also attended our church. The kids, who were not self-conscious, were our "praise the Lord section" in the church. Some people were offended by the noise but I always enjoyed their enthusiasm.

Bernie and Louise treated this group of children as a calling God had given them. When Louise got sick and needed surgery Bernie became swamped with work. I wondered what I could do to bring some relief to them.

As I thought about it the Lord prompted me to have them in for Sunday lunch. I told my husband Harold but he was not excited about it all and said no that it wasn't a good idea. Harold did not like to socialize at the best of times let alone with company that could be challenging to manage and he also said I had enough work to do already and didn't need to add another thing to my list.

As I was cleaning the house I prayed about it and felt even more convicted that I needed to do this. I planned the menu for lunch and checked to see if I had enough dishes. An hour later for some reason Harold changed his mind and gave me the permission to go ahead, with the condition that he would not be involved in any way. He also said if they would leave the house damaged I would have to find a way to pay for it. One of the boys had a reputation for peeling wallpaper off of walls and we had a lot of wallpaper in those days! I knew Harold was concerned about that.

I phoned Bernie to invite them over and his response was, "Do you know what kind of kids we are looking after?" I said yes. He said they would love to come.

I prepared more than a quick lunch as I prepared a dinner, with tablecloths, fine dinnerware and good dishes in the dining room and kitchen. I tried to make it as attractive as possible so very special!

Sunday after church the van arrived with Bernie and the ten kids. He was gentle but firm and had things in control. They all walked into the house but when Bernie saw how I had set the table he asked if I wanted to reconsider the dining room set up.

I told him, "No, all will be well."

The children were lovely and extremely well behaved, grateful and very warm towards me. Everything went well with the meal and there were no broken dishes, no mess on the floor and all the wallpaper remained on the walls! After lunch some went outside where the yard was unfinished as there was no lawn yet. They were so careful that they didn't even bring any dirt into the house. They created no damage anywhere at all and they stayed until almost 6:00 p.m.

I got a lot of hugs and kisses at the end of the day. These children showed their gratitude without holding back and that was a reward in itself! Later when they would see me in church they would come running to greet me. I hadn't expected to get more than I gave!

I learned a lesson: when God asks me to do something that could be a disaster humanly speaking or, at the very least, uncomfortable, I need not worry as God will look after every detail and I just need to be obedient to what He is asking me to do. I am so thankful that He allowed me to experience what I did that day and many other times over the years.

For pushing me out of my comfort zone and showing me how beautiful it can be there, I give thanks.

9. AN EDUCATION

"You light a lamp for me. The Lord, my God, lights up my darkness."

Psalm 18:28

* * *

After our daughter Teresa graduated from high school she decided to attend a Bible school in Saskatchewan and many graduates her age did. However, several weeks before the beginning of the semester she didn't have peace about it and decided instead to attend Fraser Valley College in Abbotsford.

Everyone had an opinion on what she should or should not do and most friends and relatives who talked to me thought she should attend Bible School first. They couldn't understand her sudden change of heart. I think people saw it as a hasty and un-thought-through decision. When I talked to Teresa I sensed that

God was leading her in her decision and that I should stand by her. I felt God was up to something.

I committed her decision to the Lord and trusted that even if it was the wrong decision, He would make something right out of it.

She enrolled in the College but it was a late enrollment so she was on the waiting list for every class. The first day of classes was just around the corner and she was not yet accepted into any of them! Then, at the last minute, she got all the courses she needed and I began to see that this was indeed the right choice for her.

What became clear about that year was that God was using it to stretch and challenge her in what she believed. Instead of undermining her beliefs it was a strengthening time for her as she put feet to her faith. She was even asked to comment on a small portion of scripture in her English class and present it to the entire class. When she did, she took her Bible along and read from it making comments and answering questions from the class.

It was such a growing year for her. She loved being able to stand up for what she believed and I praised God for it. She was strong in her convictions and we had many long conversations about various issues and I am thankful to God for the wisdom He gave me and for Teresa's willingness to listen and discuss matters in a loving caring way.

That year at college was a good year. Praise the Lord!

From there we began talking about her attending Trinity Western University in Langley, B.C. Trinity seemed like an impossibility! It was so expensive! However I felt convinced that

Teresa needed to attend there. I thought it would be good for her to make new friends and study in the wholesome environment. I prayed about it and discussed matters with Harold and Teresa and decided to proceed; God would provide.

Teresa paid half and we paid half and even though financially it wasn't easy, it was an excellent year for us all. All our lives were enriched! God provided good roommates and friends for Teresa.

Sometimes indecision means there is a better plan God is leading us to. There was no obvious reason Teresa shouldn't have gone to Bible school, yet I believe God was directing her to change her mind.

For leading us to change our mind about things for our own good, I give thanks.

10. CRANBERRIES

"The Lord protects those of childlike faith; I was facing death, and he saved me. Let my soul be at rest again, for the Lord has been good to me."

Psalm 116:6-7

* * *

When we lived in Richmond I got a kidney infection. I have always responded poorly to medication, my left kidney was already very small due to infections over the years and the condition I was experiencing had become chronic. I was referred to the surgeon for the purpose of possible removal of the kidney. Not only was the timing bad *(Harold had just recovered from a home accident and was in between jobs)* but I felt I simply could not go through with a major surgery.

Many people began to pray for us and I felt it!

One night when I could not sleep because of the pain I went downstairs to the family room and I said to God that I believed He could heal me without surgery. I believed that He was in the room and, even though I could not see him, just a word from Him would do it. I saw examples of this in Scripture and believed Jesus was the same today as He was then.

One day soon after, a neighbor of ours who was a chiropractor and a member of our church, came over and said that he had read somewhere years ago that raw cranberry juice sometimes cured kidney infections and it might be worthwhile trying. I wondered if this was an answer to my prayers as miracles come in different ways after all. Sometimes God heals instantly, sometimes through the skilled hands of a gifted Physician and perhaps through something as unexpected as cranberries.

After a persistent search for cranberries we found some. I blended the cranberries with some water, strained out the pulp and drank it. Was it ever tart! I added some sugar to begin with but over time used less and less to the point where I didn't need any at all.

Three days later I went to see the surgeon and the infection was totally gone. I had pain in the kidney for several months after but drinking the cranberry juice every day kept me healthy. After that we bought a second freezer and 300 pounds of raw cranberries from a Richmond farmer so that I could continually make fresh juice to drink.

The doctors were amazed that ten years later I still had my kidneys and still took no traditional medication. To this day, I have had only minimal complications with my kidneys; they have just kept limping along! Those cranberries have kept me healthy for over thirty years so I kept drinking the juice and as a result I always kept infection away.

Many, many times when I was picking up cranberries people would ask, "What are all those cranberries for?" I would tell them the story and they would say, "I should try that." Not that one remedy works for everyone, but maybe it was helpful to some.

What a good lesson I learned, to keep my ear open, because you never know who God is going to use to help. I praise God for the miracle performed as He sent my neighbor my way to give me a good word!

For still being the God who heals, I give thanks.

11. SUMMERTIME PRAYERS

"I cry out to the Lord; I plead for the Lord's mercy. I pour out my complaints before him and tell him all my troubles. When I am overwhelmed, you alone know the way I should turn."

Psalm 142

* * *

Before each summer came I wondered how it could best be spent. I prayed that it would be both enjoyable and productive for our children, and especially for Lloyd. My husband, Harold had a very difficult time connecting with the children as he was not affectionate and did not tell the children he loved them or was proud of them. He was very distant, often lost in a book he was reading, critical and uninvolved in their lives. It was Lloyd who seemed to suffer more than Teresa from Harold's lack of attention.

This deeply concerned me and I worked hard at filling Lloyd's life with good things, even though a father's love can never be replaced. I wanted to make sure he had great memories, and would also develop a good sense of self-worth. What Lloyd needed was an extension of our family and the example of other adults to follow.

Oh how I prayed to my heavenly Father for this; bringing Lloyd to His attention over and over again. God was so faithful in answering my prayers and providing great opportunities for Lloyd.

- ☐ My sister Hildegarde, and her husband Henry, had him over many weeks for several summer so he could take swimming lessons and play with their children. Lloyd absolutely LOVED going over to their home and their children took such good care of him. One summer Henry even provided a job for Lloyd in his store, patiently guiding Lloyd along, advising him, and helping him to develop a good work ethic.

- ☐ One summer he went to the interior of British Columbia with my brother Jake and his wife Helen for several weeks. He came back with a load of great stories from their adventure.

- ☐ For several summers my youngest brother John and his wife Heidi shared their summer home at Shuswap with Lloyd where he could run wild, swim every day, catch frogs and snakes and chase chipmunks. It was fun from morning until night!

- ☐ Even our neighbors got involved with Lloyd inviting him along to their home on the Island.

- ☐ He also went to Columbia Bible Camp *(now Stillwood)* for a week several summers.

Lloyd was a very creative boy and so when he was home I made sure he always had a lot of nails, wood, paint, and scraps of this and that to build forts and go-carts and whatever else he might dream up. Lloyd was seldom bored and full of ideas and that was always interesting to the other children who would come by to see if they could get involved too!

I also made sure Lloyd helped around the house. Here too Lloyd applied his imagination! We had a riding lawn mower and from about the age of ten and for many years after, he mowed the lawns. But Lloyd didn't just mow as he took our wagon and made it into what looked like a caboose attaching it to the mower and giving kids rides as he mowed. That made him pretty popular in the neighborhood!

The lesson I was learning was how God takes an interest in our children. He looked after Lloyd and brought people his way who would open up his world to new possibilities. Sometimes our own situations are not ideal but that doesn't mean God can't still work in those times and give us everything we need.

I am also thankful that God helped me to see Lloyd for who he was as a creative individual with so much potential. God was always giving me ideas to give Lloyd ideas and in this I can see God's tenderness and how His promise is true that He creates families for people without one. God gave Lloyd fathers to look up to when his own didn't seem to know how to engage with him.

For being a father to the "fatherless," I give thanks.

12. Six Lessons

"For I know the plans I have for you," says the Lord. "They are plans for good and not for disaster, to give you a future and a hope. In those days when you pray, I will listen. If you look for me wholeheartedly, you will find me."

Jeremiah 29:11-13

* * *

In the Spring of 1988 I noticed when Harold and I went for walks that not all was well with his heart. After tests he was referred to a heart specialist and was told he would need by-pass surgery. The waiting list was long and we were told that even if he would get called his surgery could be cancelled due to someone else needing it more.

We were in the middle of wedding plans for Teresa, which made things busy. She was also working in Vancouver and driving in with Harold. These two things gave me great concern. Planning a wedding is stressful, and we had already put in a lot of planning and money and didn't want to postpone it. I was also concerned about her driving with Harold when his heart was not working well. I was worried about her safety on the road. Harold began to feel uneasy about this heart and with the wedding near at hand we inquired if he could go to Victoria for surgery but we got nowhere with that request.

I was getting very tired and I prayed that God would at least take Harold into the hospital so that he would be in a safe place and not collapse while driving.

God answered my prayer.

One day after work he called and said that he didn't feel well and wondered if he should go to the hospital. I said he should but not to drive. I told him to call our son Lloyd or take a taxi. Lloyd took him to the hospital and they kept him in and so came the first lesson.

My first lesson? When we pray, even if we have already been told no by people, God can turn that into a yes. God does not abide by anyone's schedule. He opened the door for Harold, His way.

During his stay in the hospital Lloyd spent many hours at his bedside, which was a godsend. A lot of good conversations happened between Lloyd and his father; necessary conversations and healing conversations.

My second lesson? God uses adverse situations for His purposes. His ways are higher than our ways and are always about accomplishing good. In this case, the mending of a strained father and son relationship.

FOR WHAT WE ARE ABOUT TO RECEIVE

So many people were good to us during this time. I phoned the prayer chain and requested that they pray for surgery to happen in good time for the wedding and for a successful surgery. Many people began praying immediately.

Good friends and family stepped in to help. They offered to take me to the hospital and did many times so that I didn't need to drive. People brought meals, sent cards, called me, and tried to relieve the stress in any way possible. They ran errands related to the wedding and just carried me through this time.

One day I felt I was under a spiritual attack. Everything seemed to be going wrong with one thing after another within a matter of a couple of hours. I promptly phoned my neighbor, Dorothy, to ask her to pray for me and for my protection and she did. I don't know what the enemy was trying to do but I clearly felt that he was trying to shake me up. Thank goodness for a good neighbor who could hold me up in prayer!

With concerns on one hand for Harold and joy for Teresa on the other I often felt torn in two. But God was faithful to me. The verse I often reminded myself of was, *"I have set the Lord always before me, because he is at my right hand, I will not be shaken"* *(Psalm 16:8).*

The third lesson I learned? God uses community to bless us. So often people keep things to themselves rather than allowing others to come alongside, as they can. When we allow others to help us we are blessed and so are they!

During this most difficult time I was also praying to God for Lloyd's salvation. Lloyd had really wandered and was not living life God's way. Then just before Teresa's wedding, Lloyd committed his life to the Lord. That week *(Harold was already home from the hospital at that point)* I made a celebration dinner and expressed my gratitude to God for his mercy and for Lloyd's recommitment.

My fourth lesson? What we are walking through is not often just what it seems. God is not just about our personal comfort, He is ultimately about salvation. If it took all of this to help bring Lloyd back into right relationship with Jesus, it was all worth it.

During these months of wedding preparations and Harold's illness, the Lord sent people to me on a regular basis either by phone or in person who were hurting in various ways themselves. We talked, I listened, and we prayed. The Lord made clear to me the importance of taking past experiences and learning from them in order to know how to help others. Past experiences with God have given me confidence in trusting Him and not my own understanding. I also learned that God expects me to be available at all times, even in times when I feel needy.

My fifth lesson? We don't always know what we are capable of. With God's help we can continue to serve even when life seems overwhelming.

Twice Harold was scheduled for surgery and got bumped. Finally after a week and a half of waiting a much- needed surgery was performed three weeks before Teresa's wedding. God undertook for him in a special way. He had a quadruple-bypass surgery and recovered very well. After a week, he was back home and his recovery was remarkable. He was able to walk Teresa down the church aisle and give a great speech at the wedding reception.

My sixth lesson? God answered our prayers. His timing is always right. He gives healing and strength.

For giving me an extra measure of strength on so many different occasions I give thanks.

13. A Miraculous Healing

"Such a prayer offered in faith will heal the sick,
and the Lord will make you well."

James 5:15

* * *

In the last story I described how, at age 40, Harold had already experienced several heart attacks and it had finally came to the point where the doctor's said he would need open heart surgery. Teresa was within months of getting married and Harold was in the hospital waiting for the surgery and added to all that, I was experiencing severe bleeding *(heavy menstruation)*. Over a period of ten years I had to endure many medical procedures to try to deal with it, which helped temporarily but did not fix it. Bleeding so much left me drained and terribly uncomfortable.

I went to the doctor and he said I would need a hysterectomy soon. Not only was this inconvenient but surgery was dangerous for me since I had already had two major surgeries and my kidney function was not good on top of it all.

When I got home from the doctor's I cried out to God. I said to Him,

"God, you made a woman to have periods and you can also stop them! I am asking you for a miracle!"

I prayed as simply as that, believing God could do it. I got up, went to the bathroom, threw out my pads and I never needed to use one again. God answered my prayer immediately.

Like the story in the Bible about a woman who had a bleeding problem who touched Jesus believing He would help her, I learned He is still the same and for this I give thanks.

14. Urgency To Pray At Night

"And the Holy Spirit helps us in our weakness. For example, we don't
know what God wants us to pray for. But the Holy Spirit prays for us with
groanings that cannot be expressed in words."

Romans 8:26

* * *

The call to pray does not always happen at the most convenient
times. Many times I have been nudged awake and realize I am to
pray. It took me a while to figure this out though. I would wake
up and wonder why in the world I was up and eventually think,
"Maybe I should pray."

One night I woke up from a sound sleep and was wide-awake.
I got up and had a drink of water and went back to bed but I
still couldn't sleep. I got up again and went into the living room
and decided to pray. I started to pray for different people and

then for my dear sister Hildegarde. When I began to pray for her I suddenly felt a special burden to pray for her as I never sensed before!

After I finished praying for her I felt sleepy again and so I stopped praying and went back to bed and slept. The next day I went for a walk with Hildegarde and she told me that at night she had suddenly awakened with a most severe headache such as she had never experienced before and it was so painful that she had feared the worst. But then, all at once, it left her. When I asked her what time that was I discovered it was around the time I prayed for her.

This experience heightened my awareness that even at night the ministry of prayer must continue. I must be sensitive for that call to prayer.

Another time I had a dream in which I had a most terrible pain in my leg. I woke up suddenly with my heart pounding severely. The first thought that came to me was to pray for my brother Jake who had Parkinson's disease. I immediately got up and went into the living room and prayed specifically for him. A few days later I talked with his wife Helen and told her of my experience. She was very moved by it and said, "That must be why we had so much better a night."

Again, it encouraged me to take the prompting to pray seriously.

One night I was suddenly wide-awake and immediately asked God who I needed to pray for. This time I sensed it was for Mike and Teresa's safety.

The next morning Teresa told me that police had pursued a person down their street and around their place and had caught him in their front yard! I thanked God for alerting me to prayer and for their protection.

The lesson I learned along the way was to pay attention to those times when I seemed to wake up for "no reason." I have woken up many times at night only to find a specific name on my heart. I take some time to pray for that person and though I don't always know the outcome, I trust that these are necessary prayers and that God is at work as I pray.

When God awakens me I always feel privileged to be able to partner with Him and for this I give thanks.

15. The Right Place at The Right Time

"Be still in the presence of the Lord, and wait patiently for him to act."

Psalm 37:7

* * *

At one point it became increasingly clear that we were to move again, this time from Surrey to Abbotsford, B.C. Teresa was going to high school there and had several more years to go and I strongly felt we should be there to make it easier for her to be involved in activities after school. At the same time I wasn't sure how we would work out all the details.

After praying about it I approached Harold and we came to a decision to complete some of the unfinished projects around our house and put it up for sale. We looked at house plans and planned our own from scratch and we looked at the possibilities of building but we couldn't come to any conclusions. If we couldn't agree on a house plan we felt that God had a readymade house for us.

When the house finally sold after quite a few months we promptly phoned my nephew who was in real estate and asked him to find a few houses to show us at a certain price. I prayed that we wouldn't have to move twice and I prayed the dates we would need to move out of our present house and into our new house would work out well. I also prayed that we would live near to the school Teresa was attending and that the house would be basically finished.

My nephew showed us around Abbotsford but we found nothing. There wasn't a single house that was right. Near the end of the day we were looking in a subdivision I quite liked but did not find a suitable house. The subdivision was in the perfect location so it puzzled me that we had not found the right house.

We were getting ready to go back to his office to think about what to do next and I felt a prompting and I said to him, "Are you sure you don't have one more house?" I had no sooner said that when he spotted a "For Sale" sign on a house which had just been put up. We drove to his office for a key and particulars, looked at it, talked about it, drove away and went back again.

I knew immediately that it was the one but I said nothing for or against.

On the way back to the office he said, "So what have you decided Aunt Violet?"

"It's the one," I said, then added "...but of course I have to consult Uncle Harold."

We all laughed that I was so certain.

The dates were right, the price was right, the location was right, and it was totally finished. It even had a free-standing wood stove *(the kind we had previously and had enjoyed)*.

After we moved in our real estate agent from Surrey phoned and said that our deal in Surrey may be collapsing because of a clause that said the new owners could not put up a fence. We knew nothing about the clause. There was no way we would be able to carry two mortgages and so I was back to praying again!

The real estate agent felt I was telling the truth about the matter and she took things in hand and went to the city hall in Surrey to try to overthrow the ruling. God was with her and gave her success; the officials cooperated and all turned out well.

The lesson I learned is that God is in the details. He knows exactly what we need and how to lead us towards it but we need to ask Him for it, trust Him, and not side-step Him in the process. God knew where the right house would be and He worked everything out for us and He turned a potentially bad situation into a positive one.

For God who has always put a roof over my head I give thanks.

16. The Lost Earrings

"The Lord directs the steps of the godly.
He delights in every detail of their lives."

Psalm 37:23 NLT

* * *

One Christmas Harold gave me some expensive and beautiful earrings. We did not often give each other gifts at Christmas but for some reason he really wanted to get something for me that year. His effort made those earrings special to me and I wore them almost every day.

One day I was mowing the lawn. I felt quite warm and decided to remove an outer layer of clothes. I stopped the mower and proceeded to take my long-sleeved shirt off over my head. As I did so I hooked one of my earrings, and it went flying somewhere.

I looked in the dry, brown and green grass and couldn't find it since it blended in color and was quite small.

I looked for such a long time and simply could not see it. I was hot and sweaty and concerned. I am normally a very practical person and not terribly sentimental, but I really valued that gift from my husband. So I prayed that I would find it. Maybe that seems silly, but that is what I did, and have done so many times.

As I squatted down once more I suddenly lost my balance! I put my hand out to steady myself and as I did so my little finger touched something hard. It was my earring. I smiled at this because it was just so kind of God to help me. Once again in my weakness *(losing my balance),* He proved He could help me with any little or big thing.

Those earrings became known as the "lost earrings" because I lost and found them so many times over the years. Once, one of them even landed in a huge pile of sawdust and I was able to still retrieve it! I am not sure why this has happened so often but maybe it is simply to show me God's graciousness again and again.

Perhaps that is the lesson, that God cares about what we care about, even the small, material things in life. For this I give thanks.

17. A Witness

"I urge you, first of all, to pray for all people. Ask God to help them; intercede on their behalf, and give thanks for them."

1 Timothy 2:1

* * *

I always wanted my children to know what it looked like to reach out to a neighbor. Harold was not very sociable and did not really enjoy having people in. He wasn't one to naturally connect with people and so that left it up to me.

One year some new neighbors moved in next door to us and I got to know them. It became evident that they did not know Jesus and that there were a lot of problems they were dealing with. Christmas was coming and the neighbors I had invited to our annual church banquet turned us down so I thought I would give the tickets back to the church. However God prompted me to invite the new neighbors to be our guests.

I was apprehensive as I didn't know them well but I told Harold about my conviction and he told me to go ahead and invite them if I wanted to. I really thought they wouldn't come and God was only testing my obedience. I phoned them and they said they would love to come!

It was a lovely evening but the speaker, who was normally a very good speaker, spoke for a long time! He spoke for a whole hour! Our guests kept looking at their watches and at each other and I thought, "They are bored and will never come again to anything in this church!"

When the speaker prayed and explained the way of salvation, I couldn't help but notice them holding hands and looking at each other and I knew the seed of God's conviction had been planted. On the way home they said, "Well, we think we should send our children to Sunday School, what do you think? It might be good for them."

Without really thinking I said that was not a good idea. Children become very confused if the parents don't go. Why would it be important for the children and not for their parents? They thanked us for the good evening and said that they would think about what we had talked about.

The next morning was Sunday and I got a call from our neighbors asking if they and their children could come with us to church. They had been married in a church and had attended a few times here and there they told us. We said we would take them and I had them in for lunch later.

God gave me such a love for them!

From then on they all attended church regularly whenever their jobs allowed it. I approached several people in the church and also our neighbors down the street who worked with Youth For Christ to consider if God was calling them to befriend our neighbors and help them along....and they did.

After a number of months both became Christians. Life didn't just become easy for them though. The devil tried his best to destroy their relationship with each other and God. But God kept them in His sight. It was so exciting to see their childlike faith and how they prayed with such sincerity. They attended a new Believer's class and truly came out of the kingdom of darkness into the kingdom of light.

They were the only ones in their families who were Christians and they had no role models so when Harold and I moved to Abbotsford they moved too! They attended the church we attended there as well. We kept in touch and I had many opportunities to help and encourage them and I saw how they were reaching out to others and encouraging them too! It was beautiful.

Over the years I welcomed new neighbors into our different neighborhoods with loaves of homemade bread, took care of their children, invited them over for coffee and tried as much as possible to be hospitable. I am so thankful for the opportunities God gave me to extend the hand of friendship to neighbors.

I have never been the most outgoing person, a person who easily engages others in conversation, but I was willing to be stretched as a follower of Jesus. I wanted to do this in obedience to God but I also wanted to do this to disciple my children. So even though it didn't always come naturally, I know God used my efforts.

For giving me opportunities to live out the Gospel like this I give thanks.

18. COMFORT OTHERS

"He comforts us in all our troubles so that we can comfort others. When they are troubled, we will be able to give them the same comfort God has given us."

2 Corinthians 1:4

* * *

At one point my husband's father was in the hospital and was on the waiting list for an extended care home. While in intensive care, he commented that he was in despair. I heard him, prayed for him and then told Harold and the others over supper that his comment could not be ignored. There was something going on that was making Grandpa uneasy and we needed to "do battle" on his behalf.

Since we were all busy during the day we asked a friend of Grandpa's whether he could regularly visit him during the day and care for him and pray over him. They spent considerable time together and it was helpful to him.

I also felt that every time we visited Grandpa we should read scripture to him and pray even though, at this point, he didn't appear to notice and was agitated a lot of the time. I am sure he didn't mean to be, but he was not feeling well and it made him unhappy.

It bothered my husband Harold that his father was this way. He found it stressful being with him and suggested we shouldn't visit quite so often. This was Harold's family and I didn't want to push him but when the next day came around, I felt very strongly that we needed to go and see him again and comfort him when he needed it the most.

As we walked in the next evening he surprised us as he immediately urged us to read Scripture and pray for him.

"Hurry Up. Do it <u>now</u>!" He said.

I really felt at that point we were helping Harold's father *"walk through the valley of the shadow of death"* that the Bible speaks of. It was a difficult time for him and we needed to help him in this part of his journey.

After we had read and prayed we helped make him comfortable, and he told us we could leave. That night he passed away in his sleep. We went to the hospital to say goodbye and it was a very special moment.

I have walked with a lot of people when they weren't their best and the lesson I have learned along the way is to extend care anyway. I learned to look past what I saw or heard especially when they were in a weak or irritable condition. I learned that I might not always have just the right words and that I might not be able to solve the problem. I might even feel inadequate for the task but prayer is the one thing I could always offer out loud or silently. No matter who anyone is, or whatever condition they might be in, I can bring every person before God and ask for His help on their behalf.

That has always made me feel strong in the power of God, courageous before His throne, and helpful even while on the outside I look quiet.

I can pray with confidence knowing that as soon as those words are even a thought, God is already acting and for this I give thanks.

19. ACCIDENTAL LESSON

"I know the Lord is always with me.
I will not be shaken, for he is right beside me."

Psalm 16:8

* * *

We were planning to go camping, it was summer and it was hot outside. I was on my way to Teresa's place around noon and had come to a stop at the red light with several cars ahead of me. When the light turned green I began to drive when I noticed that there was a problem up ahead. I was prepared to stop quickly which is what I had to do. Suddenly, I found my car being pushed into the car ahead of me with quite a jolt! The driver behind me, which happened to be my neighbor, wasn't paying attention as she had looked down while shifting gears and slammed into me.

She admitted she was at fault. My car had to have some repair but more troublesome was the injury I had sustained to my neck and shoulder. The impact of being hit from behind had done put something out of place and I found myself waking up at night, in pain. The doctor recommended physiotherapy and this lasted for months.

All this would have been fine; things happen and it wasn't the worst thing in the world. But then I began having problems with the neighbor who had hit me. She felt I couldn't possibly have been hurt in the accident! She took it upon herself to phone ICBC, defend herself and complain about me. She said I wasn't injured from the accident. She actually came to our house at night with her husband to look under our car to see if the damage was as bad as ICBC was saying!

I didn't know what to do about it but my doctor was very firm with me and told me not to settle with ICBC until he gave the okay as I had an injury that would need attention for some time. It was so stressful and as uncomfortable as I was at night, I was even more uncomfortable with my angry neighbor! I sure didn't like being at odds with anyone. Added to that my medical expenses were mounting and during the year we had some other unforeseen expenses that put extra pressure on us.

As I was quiet before God I knew He was calling me to be kind to my neighbor even when she was unkind. She created so much tension between us yet I knew God was just telling me to be loving in spite of her ridicule. Between dealing with the police, the repair shop and the ICBC agents and alongside my appointments over the course of the year, God was saying to just extend kindness over and over. I did this.

I wish I could say, at the end of it all that my neighbor turned around, that we ended up being best friends and it was all worth it! That never happened. Relating with my neighbor was an incredibly stretching experience and I have no idea how my being persistently kind affected her. I can say that it definitely did something to me as it taught me how to give love even if it was never returned and to be kind even if that kindness wasn't even appreciated.

As I look back, what I received from that accident was good.

And then, God actually blessed us with just enough money from the settlement to cover all of my medical expenses and a little more to help with the needs that we wouldn't have had the finances to cover.

If I had a choice I would not have chosen to have an accident in order to have my needs met, but God knows the reasons. Who knows but that one day my neighbor will find God because of my continued friendliness to her, for showing love in a situation like that.

I acknowledge that God's ways are higher than mine and for this I give thanks

20. The Dry Floral Arrangement

"So humble yourselves before God. Resist the devil,
and he will flee from you."

James 4:7

* * *

One Christmas I started looking for a floral arrangement to be hung over a mirror in our dining room. I just simply couldn't find the right one. Then, while shopping in the mall, I noticed a display booth with beautiful arrangements. The one arrangement in particular caught my attention. I bought it and hung it up. It was beautiful and the price was very good. I was pleased.

That night before falling asleep Harold said to me, "By the way, what did you buy for $25.00?" I told him it was the floral arrangement. He said "At Witchcraft Coquitlam?" I was totally shocked at his comment. I had not noticed any sign that indicated that name and the bill was so faint it could hardly be deciphered, but there it was!

That made me uncomfortable and I prayed and told God I would never have bought it had I known who sold it. I prayed for protection over me and over the house.

The next morning I went to drive my car when I noticed that the inside mirror was turned the wrong way as it was twisted so that it was vertical instead of horizontal. I was puzzled by it since no one had driven it but me.

The following day the same thing happened again. Again, I prayed for protection.

A few days later I had a most terrifying nightmare. I woke up suddenly and sensed a presence in the room. I literally shook with fear and immediately prayed to God and became calm.

A few nights later I woke up suddenly with the strangest pain in my neck and it felt as if someone biting me! Again, I sensed a presence in the room. Frightened, I prayed and the presence left and I became calm.

The next day I told Harold I had enough and I knew what I needed to do. I took the arrangement down and stuck it in a garbage bag, stepped on it to crush it and then Harold took it to the garbage dump.

That was the end of that kind of activity!

I don't know why this particular object brought trouble; I am sure I have had many objects in my home made by people who worship many different things. I just know that there was something about this one, sold by an organization that supported witchcraft, that I needed to pay attention to.

The lesson I learned was that we always need a spirit of discernment to recognize the enemy and deal with him. Resist the devil and he will flee from you, the Bible says. Test everything. Avoid every kind of evil. Hold onto the good.

I learned that I need to have an awareness about what happens in the "supernatural" realm, not because I need to dwell on it, or fear it, but that it is real and God is greater than any evil we might encounter. I learned that there are times I needed to get rid of things that were not "right," things I shouldn't have in a God-honoring home.

Some people shrug those things off but I learned that just as there is a very real and loving God, there is also an enemy who wants to steal, kill and destroy. We should be mindful of that.

For this lesson, for opening my eyes to the "unseen," I give thanks.

21. MY MOTHER AND I

"Praise the Lord; praise God our savior!
For each day he carries us in his arms."

Psalm 68:19

* * *

My mother and I had a tumultuous relationship all along. I always found it hard to get close to her and to be myself. Our personalities differed as she was an emotional person and I was more objective. She was very sentimental and I was more "no-nonsense." It isn't that opposites can't get along, but for some reason she had a hard time letting me just be me. I was the sixth child and she almost died delivering me. She told me on more than one occasion that she hadn't wanted more children, which left me feeling unwanted. She would pick at me, never satisfied with how I did things. She would compare me to my sisters and I just couldn't meet her expectations and she certainly wouldn't compliment me because she believed that would make me proud.

This went on through my growing up years and into adulthood.

When she was older and I was, by now, married I would visit her and it seldom went well. She would be upset that I hadn't given her enough details about my day-to-day life or I hadn't stayed long enough or she would disagree with decisions we were making. If she thought I was holding something back from her she would get upset at me and hold a grudge. She would look at how I was living my life and always find something to criticize. I didn't say much about it for many years and when I did bring it up with my mother she would begin to blame me for things that she was unhappy about in her own life.

Two weeks before my mother died we had a frustrating exchange on the telephone. She had been in the hospital as her heart was bothering her and she was discharged at the doctor's recommendation. Her health was failing and we, her children, had to make some decisions about her care. It was a difficult time as mom had a hard time accepting that she needed help.

One morning during this process, she phoned me and was very angry about a list of issues and she proceeded to blame me for each problem, one by one. I listened as best I could but as it became more and more personal I finally told her that what she was doing was wrong, a sin, and very unkind. She hung up on me and wouldn't answer when I tried to reach her.

The next morning she phoned me before she had breakfast and said she had been wrong. She asked for my forgiveness. This was a first and only time she asked for forgiveness.

As we walked through this time with my mother I grieved that I could not find a way to have a close relationship with her. One day I cried for most of the day and then I came to a place of thankfulness.

- ☐ I was thankful for the love I had been shown by other people, especially Hildegarde who showed me so much "motherly" love. She had always been there in such a beautiful way when I needed her.

- ☐ I also thanked God for His unconditional love, and how much my own longing to be accepted had drawn me towards Him.

- ☐ I thanked him for my own little family and for every person over the years who had accepted me and loved me.

- ☐ I even could thank God for my mother who I did care for in spite of everything. We were both believers and even if things were imperfect now, they wouldn't always be.

When she died with most of the children and their spouses present it was a strange feeling. Part of me felt angry that I had not been able to have a special mother/daughter relationship but I also felt relief and freedom for both of us. I had prayed for her so often over the years and knew that God was calling me to treat her well, even when I did not feel treated well. I never had lashed back at her even when it was hard to hold my words back. I truly wanted to honor and respect my mother.

Now, as I reflect back, I am so thankful that I listened to God about that, as I do not have any burden of guilt. I also feel joy over the fact that when we are children of God and we meet in eternity, we will be changed people, perfect in God's eyes and reconciled with one another.

It is possible to love, when not loved. It is possible to be a friend, when not befriended. It is possible to live without bitterness and blame and for this I give thanks.

22. Inheritance Money

"What is the price of five sparrows—two copper coins? Yet God does not forget a single one of them. And the very hairs on your head are all numbered. So don't be afraid; you are more valuable to God than a whole flock of sparrows."

Luke 12:6

* * *

Several months after my mother died my siblings and I were given some of the inheritance money she had left us. I don't know why, but I felt strongly that I should not spend any of it, but put it into a GIC (Guaranteed Investment Certificate), which I did. I strongly felt it needed to be an emergency fund; though for what emergency I was not sure.

Little did I know that this was to be a very important move!

Less than one year later, Harold passed away without warning and I needed instant cash to pay the bills before the insurance money would come in. The GIC was there, ready to be used for that purpose.

So many times, especially as a widow, I would feel this sudden urge that I should do something, and to others it might not even have made sense. I couldn't always explain it, but I knew God was preparing me for something down the line. He has taken care of me time after time in this way: protecting me, providing for me, preparing me for some new thing.

Over the years I really have come to "know God's voice" and trust that nudge or prompt, knowing He is preparing the way in advance.

God sees the future and has given me excellent advice and for this I give thanks.

23. Harold's Passing

"You will keep in perfect peace all who trust in you, all whose thoughts are fixed on you!"

Isaiah 26:3

* * *

Harold was scheduled to go to New York on a business trip. I did not feel good about him going as I just simply did not have peace about it and couldn't really explain why. I sensed that something was not right with his health even though he had no heart related pain. When I asked him to change his mind about going he became quite annoyed with me. I thought and prayed about this a while sensing his mind was made up, and asked God what I should do about my unease. God made it clear to me.

I went to Harold and said if he was set on going, I would appreciate it if he would take out extra insurance, which he did. I then asked him if he would update me on all financial matters and write it all down which he did also. He really thought I was over-reacting, but I knew something wasn't right.

A day before he was to leave he phoned me from the office and said he was just too busy to go since his "second in command" had to fly to London to see his mother who was very sick. He cancelled his flight and hotel reservation. He would postpone his trip to New York for now. I felt a tremendous sense of relief. I also thought about the extra insurance we purchased and all the work on the finances I had asked Harold to do, and wondered if I had made him do a lot of work for nothing.

Later, after supper we went for a walk and we met our neighbor outside and he invited us in and we talked for a long while. That was the last thing Harold and I did together.

The next day I was watching the news at noon and having my lunch. There was something on the news that made me concerned for Harold's safety. I don't know what it was but I remember turning the TV off and just really praying for him and for some other concerns I had about our marriage and my own future.

Shortly after one o clock I went upstairs to do some work when the phone rang. It was approximately 1:15 p.m. It was a co-worker's of Harold's. He told me Harold had collapsed, it didn't look good and that I should phone the Burnaby General Hospital right away.

My heart beat terribly and jumped all over the place. I thought I would collapse! I phoned the hospital and was told it did not look good.

"Are you alone?" they asked

I said, "Yes."

"Maybe you should have someone come with you. Don't drive alone," they said.

I said I wouldn't.

Though I didn't know it at that point Harold had collapsed at the Sky-train on the way to a job. He was getting off the train, walking behind his colleagues and had a massive heart-attack and died instantly.

I called the children and Harold's mother and we all went to the hospital. When we got there they gave us his messed up clothes *(his shirt had been shredded while a medical team tried to revive him)*, his briefcase and other personal belongings. Harold's boss was there and we talked to him about what had happened. Finally the doctor met with us and confirmed, though they had tried to revive him, that Harold had died.

We picked up Harold's truck, which was parked at the sky train parking lot and drove to the White Spot restaurant and had supper. Harold loved eating at the White Spot and we would often go there on a Friday night. After supper I opened Harold's wallet and there was just enough cash to pay for our supper and a tip! I raised my glass and Harold's wallet and I said, "One last meal on dad."

As I reflected on what had happened I praised God that Harold had not suffered, that he had not been alone when he died, and that it hadn't happened while he had been driving. Even though our marriage had been challenging I knew I would miss Harold's companionship, and I didn't know what the future would look like for me..... but I knew God would lead me. I praised Him for giving me a warning that Harold should not go to New York as a premonition that something was going to happen and that I had acted upon it.

Without knowing what was ahead, Harold had prepared for my future with the extra life insurance and by laying out all I needed to know with the finances. For this I give thanks.

24. Isn't There Something More?

"My purpose is to give them a rich and satisfying life."

John 10:10

* * *

Some time before Harold died I had felt an increasing emptiness and restlessness in my life. I felt like there was something more for me but didn't know what this meant. I felt there should be more meaning and purpose for me but I didn't know what to do with all of that.

I suppose some people try to find answers in other ways, and sometimes in destructive things but I knew there would be nothing to satisfy me except for what God would direct me to do and be.

Then one day I sat down after lunch and cried out to God and asked Him for direction. I asked, "Is this all You have for me?"

It was only minutes later that I received the call that something had happened to my husband Harold. I would find out a short while later that he had died.

What was God up to? I was soon to find out.

Ten months later I came up to Kelowna with Michael and Teresa to start a church. My grandson Nathan was only a few days old and the other three were also very young. I felt a real calling to go with them and serve God in whatever capacity I was needed. God directed me to do this and to go as a "missionary" and an "armor bearer" to my family and to that community.

I packed my things, sold my home, and rolled up my sleeves!

Fifteen years later, and I can honestly say that these have been some of the most <u>fulfilling</u> and <u>rewarding</u> years of my life.

I found out that God indeed had something more for me. As difficult as it was to think about the future as a widow, had Harold not died at that time, I would not have been able to serve God in this way. God uses everything for His good and our good and He goes before us and for this I give thanks.

25. THE HANDKERCHIEF

"God places the lonely in families; he sets the prisoners free and gives them joy."

Psalm 68:6

* * *

Some months after Harold died, I was at a church service in Abbotsford where I lived at the time. Early on in the service I realized it was Mother's Day. The pastor called the men in the room to recognize the special women in their life, whether it be their wife or their mother, by standing with them and giving them a big hug.

Everyone stood and hugged someone they were with. I remained seated as I was there on my own.

Nearby, a young man noticed me. He walked up to me and said, "Would you mind if I would give you a hug?"

I was surprised and said, "I would love that."

I stood and the young man gave me a big hug, the kind a son would give.

I began to cry as he walked away, and found I could not stop crying! It had been so beautiful to me to have someone I didn't even know see my need and want to offer such kindness.

An older couple sat nearby and the woman came to me and pulled a handkerchief from her purse and offered it to me. I could see that it must have been a gift. It was embroidered with the words, "There is no dearer friend than a sister."

I said, "I can't take this as I have a feeling it is something special to you."

The woman said, "It is. That is why I want you to have it, sister."

That made me cry all the more but this time I had the handkerchief to dry my tears.

The lesson in that was clear to me. The church is a place where the lonely find family. Sisters are not just the naturally born ones but they are the ones Christ binds together in Christian love through His idea, the Church.

I had known that but there in my grief was a wonderful example of it. I have often thought back on that especially when I see people who look lonely. When I see someone sitting on their own at church I make a point of going to them and sitting and talking with them.

We are called to notice people and to move beyond our personal sense of space and what is "proper" to love, no matter your age and no matter what you know or don't know about a person.

For giving us the "Church," my extended family, I give thanks.

26. THE DECISION TO MOVE

"So I say, let the Holy Spirit guide your lives."

Galatians 5:16

* * *

What will we put "on the line" for God? Will we journey through this life simply for our own gain whatever that might be? Will we simply seek to improve our lives and perhaps some of this along the way will affect others positively? Or will we surrender what we consider "ours" for a greater purpose?

I have had to wrestle with these questions as I have considered what it means to truly be a "follower" of Jesus. That word does not sound very stationary to me.

Ten months after my husband Harold died, my son-in-law Mike and daughter Teresa were moving to West Kelowna to plant a church and they said to me, "Mom, come to Kelowna with us and be a part of the team and let's see what God is going to do."

I opened my Bible up over the next few days and read 1 Samuel 14:6. In this story a detachment of Philistines had gone out to create problems for the Israelites. The Israelite King's son, Jonathan, and his armor-bearer decided to do some spying on the Philistines, not telling King Saul about it. In the passage, Jonathan says to his armor-bearer, "Come let's go over to the outpost of the Philistines. Perhaps the Lord will act on our behalf. Nothing can hinder the Lord from saving, whether by many or by few." His armor-bearer replied, "Do as you have in mind. Go ahead, I am with you heart and soul." Then Jonathan lays out a plan, the two fight a battle, and God gives them victory over their enemy.

As I prayed about this decision I felt called to be an armor bearer for Mike and Teresa and for this new church

- ☐ Whether I would be the armor bearer of prayer,
- ☐ Or the armor bearer of caring for their children or other people's children,
- ☐ Or the armor bearer of feeding strangers and welcoming them into our home,
- ☐ Or the armor bearer of faith.

Whatever it might be, I felt God urging me to be with them heart and soul!

But who was I? It didn't matter and all that mattered was to take God at His word and be obedient.

VIOLET NEUMANN *with Teresa Klassen*

I knew I could go because God doesn't look for perfect people before He can use them; just vulnerable, transparent, real and, yes, imperfect ones.

I could go because I knew I didn't have to know everything before I said yes. God knew the time-frame of this part of the adventure and whether it was short term or long term. I just needed to be willing.

I could go because even though it was hard to leave the comfort zone of familiar faces and voices and surroundings, God had given me the desire to be a part of a blessing and He would be my guide, my friend, and my strength.

I believe we can be useful to God from the beginning of our lives to the end. I believe that as long as we have breath we have an opportunity.

I was a widow and I didn't know clearly how my gifts could be used and I knew I would be lonely at times *(missing dear friends and siblings)*, but so what? If God had a plan for me wouldn't He bring a fulfillment and joy along with it that I couldn't ask for or imagine?

I had learned this from lessons along the way when I took God's Word to heart and put it to practice. God had always proved Himself faithful and I trusted He would and He did! The 15 years I spent with Mike and Teresa, with my church family, and in this community have been some of the most amazing years of my life. In many ways I learned who I was, I did things I never knew I was capable of, I had more joy than I ever could have thought, I met wonderful people of all ages and walks of life, and I felt so useful and loved and contented.

I praise God for all of this! For this "second life" I give thanks.

27. THE RIGHT PRICE

"When I think of all this, I fall to my knees and pray to the Father."

Ephesians 3:14

* * *

When I move to West Kelowna together with Mike and Teresa I didn't know if I would stay, but I did stay! The following Spring I met with a realtor in Abbotsford to list my house as I knew West Kelowna would be my home permanently now. He went through a lot of listings and sales statistics in our area but I already knew how much I wanted to sell it for and I told him what it was and that I was in no hurry. I had prayed about it and had a peace about where I had landed.

He pressured me to lower the listing price and my expectations. Things were very slow in real estate and he felt if I would not lower my price, the house would not sell.

I wouldn't budge.

I had already decided ahead of time that I would leave my washer and dryer if needed to satisfy the buyer, and left myself some room to go down a little bit. My realtor shook his head at me, feeling I was unrealistic and I am sure I probably was! But I felt God was leading me in this decision and I told him that I didn't want to hear any more about the poor market! If he couldn't do as I asked, I was not interested in doing business with him.

In about two weeks I had an offer. I sold the house for what I wanted, and knew God had once again taken care of me.

The lesson is that God is not bound by statistics and what the market is doing at the time. He will accomplish His purposes and answers to no one and for this I give thanks.

28. To Mexico!

"Are you tired? Worn out? Burned out on religion? Come to me. Get away with me and you'll recover your life. I'll show you how to take a real rest. Walk with me and work with me—watch how I do it. Learn the unforced rhythms of grace. I won't lay anything heavy or ill-fitting on you. Keep company with me and you'll learn to live freely and lightly."

Matthew 11:28-30, The Message

* * *

Living with my daughter's family has never been dull. We have had so many adventures together! Whenever the seven of us wanted to take a holiday on our very limited budget it was a lot of work but a lot of fun!

When the kids were small we decided to try camping. We ended up being cold and uncomfortable and we decided very quickly that tenting was not for us! After one tenting excursion we'd had enough and ended up in a hotel. Teresa managed to cook there and we all slept in one room!

Mike and Teresa then bought a tent trailer. At least now we were off the ground and the cooking arrangement were better. However there was no washroom and stepping over all the bodies on the floor to get to the outhouse was a challenge. There were a lot of funny stories that came from holidaying with the Klassen crew!

When our church was planning a youth trip to Mexico to build a house for a family in need, I knew some adults were going along as well but I had said that was not for me. However, a couple of weeks before the team left I was driving to church and God said to me that I had not even asked Him if I should go. That was true, I hadn't asked. So I said to God that if I were to go, I would need three things that would make it possible for me.

1. I needed my Passport renewal to come back. I had sent it off but it had been rejected and I wanted to have that passport. The border crossings were getting more complicated and I would have more peace if I had it.
2. I needed my travel medical to be approved and affordable.
3. And I wanted an RV for our family, so that when we went on this trip and other vacations, I could be a part of them in a little more comfort......I was a senior citizen after all! I needed one at a good price and in good shape.

When I had prayed, I felt an overwhelming joy and I knew I needed to go! I waited for God to answer. The passport came in. The travel medical was arranged. Now what about the RV?

I was working at the church campus a week later when my son-in-law Mike came in and said to me that our mechanic had told them about an older RV he had, and said that we should buy it as it was in good shape. When Mike told me this I said we should go look at it.

That evening we looked at it and saw how well it had been maintained, and I bought it!

So that was our first RV. It was a twenty-one-footer, had no extras but it served the purpose! I went to Mexico and I was safe and healthy and comfortable! We had a terrific time and I got in there with everyone else, helping with the construction, meeting the people, eating all the food and enjoying wonderful fellowship with all those young people. I am so glad I went. I had never done anything like that before!

I was so excited that I was a part of that adventure and knew I would go on many more. I learned that I shouldn't just say, "That's not for me," but to always pray about it first.

"Ask, seek and knock" that is what God asked us to do and by doing so, I have been on many adventures and for this I give a hearty thanks!

29. HEART ATTACK

"Please, God, rescue me! Come quickly, Lord, and help me."

Psalm 70:1

* * *

In 2009 it was my turn to plan and look after the Christmas dinner for my siblings. As brothers and sisters we always "rotated" who hosted the Christmas dinner. Since I lived in West Kelowna and my siblings all lived in the Vancouver area, it was decided that I would host using my sister's place in Abbotsford.

I packed up and had a huge suitcase full of caramel popcorn in bags and tins of Christmas cookies in addition to all my clothes. I took the bus that was across the bridge and about 25 minutes from our home because there was a better chance of me getting a seat from that station than from the one that was closer *(the West Kelowna station).*

No sooner was I seated on the bus and got going that I started to feel really warm and had some indigestion and I debated if I should get off at the West Kelowna station. Before I made the decision, a voice firmly said to me, "Violet, get off the bus!" I knew it must be God telling me as no one was sitting next to me.

I went to the driver and told him I wasn't feeling well and I needed to get off at the West Kelowna Station. When we got there he helped me find a seat at the station and brought me my luggage.

I phoned Teresa to come pick me up but she was on the other side of the city with my granddaughter Alecia who was getting her driver's license. I then phoned my daughter-in-law Roberta who came to get me. I just wanted to go home but Roberta told me she was taking me directly to Emergency because she thought I was having a heart attack.

Sure enough, I was having a heart attack, and within an hour I had a coronary stent put in.

The amazing thing is how God had orchestrated it all.

- ☐ Roberta had just started her practical nursing training and recognized the symptoms.
- ☐ Two weeks before, the coronary department had opened in the hospital so they could do the stent in Kelowna. If this had happened any earlier, they would have flown me to Vancouver or Victoria. Who knows how much damage would have been done if I would have had to wait for the procedure.
- ☐ One artery was completely plugged and I needed immediate attention. Since it was only nine-o-clock in the morning the doctors and medical teams were just starting the

day and were available to do the stent quickly

Teresa showed up at the hospital after an hour. She said I didn't look like I'd had a heart attack. I was sitting up in bed, chatting, looking as healthy as ever. We laughed together and just couldn't believe how good God had been to me once again, warning me and protecting me and arranging for such good care!

Meanwhile, what was to happen to my sibling's Christmas dinner? My sister's homemaker's husband was a very good chef and had a couple of days off, and so he and his wife looked after the dinner. Apparently it tasted amazing and the presentation was beautiful as well. They put all their expertise and kindness into it.

Oh how I love the whisper of God and the care He has given to me, for who am I? For this I give thanks.

30. RIDES TO AND FROM

"You see me when I travel and when I rest at home.
You know everything I do."

Psalm 139:3

* * *

This might not seem so remarkable to some, but when you are in your seventies and not very confident about driving getting a ride somewhere can be a big thing!

One summer I needed to make a number of trips from West Kelowna to Abbotsford and found that summer is a difficult time to find space on the bus and if you do get on, it is often crowded and uncomfortable. So, instead of trying to take the bus, Teresa helped to make my request for rides known to people through Facebook.

I prayed about it also and all summer I got rides. Some were friends, some young adults I had hardly met, one was a neighbour and another was a cousin of Mike's. It was just so encouraging to me how people responded and how I was able to get to know people as we drove together.

The lesson *(although I had learned this one a long time ago, so by now I hardly had to think about it)* is that God loves to be involved in all the hours of our day, all our needs, all the things we have questions about. Why don't more people pray about more things?

Our God is One Who is concerned about all areas of our life, and for this I give thanks.

In Closing

Now I am 75 and I have this "bad" news that I have an incurable form of cancer. When the doctors first told me that things weren't looking good they said, "You probably have about two months to live".

I am not sure if that will be true but maybe it will be, or maybe it won't be.

I have been reading over these stories from my life and there are so many more stories of God's faithfulness, and I am amazed at this journey. God has been so faithful. He has been faithful to me all along.

These past 15 years in Kelowna have been incredible. I have never regretted moving here. These have been the years in which I discovered my spiritual gifts. I always said I didn't know what my gifts were and Kelowna gave me ample opportunities to explore my gifts and abilities. I have loved serving in whatever capacity God directed me.

I have met wonderful friends and have had rich fellowship.

I have learned to pray and intercede when the church was in good times and when we were treading in troubled waters.

I have loved living with Mike and Teresa and my grandkids. It has been wonderful to have my son Lloyd and Roberta and Levi nearby as well. I have been able to see my brothers and sisters many times throughout the year as well. How good it has been.

As the news sank in that I was ill, Teresa asked me, "Mom, are you praying for healing?"

I said, "I am praying that if God still has a job for me to do, then I know He will extend my days and give me health and strength. However, if my work is done here, then take me home! I am ready!"

If it isn't God's plan to give me health and strength here on hearth, I won't be writing any more stories. I hope this little book makes its way around and encourages others in their faith. I hope it ignites something in those who read it, that God, who is mysterious and beyond our human understanding, is also practical and personal. This has been my experience.

For what I have received from Him, I am...and I think I will understand this shortly...<u>eternally</u> thankful.

Living Well/Dying Well

By Teresa Klassen

My mother passed away on March 11, 2012 of Pancreatic Cancer. So much could be said about the past fifteen years, but what I want to reflect on here are the sixty-four days after she was diagnosed with Pancreatic Cancer and how she handled it on a personal/spiritual level.

Mom came to know Jesus and follow Him as a child and over the years she grew to know Him and love Him in a way that transformed her life. It was this relationship that helped her face her living days and her dying days so beautifully. This is what she modeled for us:

1. Be open about Dying

Mom didn't typically mince words and so she didn't "beat around the bush," so to speak. Mom could be honest but she was also humble and loving and so it worked.

On January 6th my husband Michael, son Nathan and I sat in a hospital room with mom and she told us the bad news. The doctors had told her she had cancer and it could mean two months to live. We all felt like we had been punched in the stomach, but we were also amazed at how mom was able to speak so openly about it. She had poise and presence. She was honest and, as mom always was, she was direct.

From then on there was no tip-toeing around the subject. We never needed to ease into what might have been the uncomfortable conversations associated with dying and it was completely acceptable to discuss it. I would look at mom while we talked and I could see that she had complete peace in her eyes. At times I would ask, "Is this uncomfortable for you?" and she assured me she was just fine.

After she passed away I sifted through her journals and there I read her spiritual reflections about life and death and it was completely evident that over the years she had developed a confidence that she was in God's hands, in life or death. No wonder she was such an open book. She had lived this way – learning to trust God with everything and being open was a natural response to how she had learned and lived.

Jesus spoke openly about his dying. Matthew 16:21 says Jesus began to show His disciples that he would suffer and be killed and He kept bringing it up! Following His lead, if He talked about it, why shouldn't she?

Mom's approach to the news was so helpful because the topic was open and on the table. Whether it was with her children, her grandchildren, friends and even strangers, mom seemed to want to allow people to talk to her about this mysterious thing called "death" and "eternity." She felt an obligation to do it, like it was a last gift she could give.

All of us were able to talk to her about what she was feeling and what she was thinking about along the way. We had terrific and unflinching conversations about life and death. Mom didn't let us pretend either and as she was dying, there were practical things to talk about.

When we discussed the topic of her "pending" memorial we ended up writing her life-story together. I asked her, "Are you ok with this, with me talking about you in the past tense?" She was (I cried more than her). We went through pictures together and took care of practical business together. Mom never hid.

When she struggled she talked about this too. We prayed with her, cried with her, hugged her, and admitted what was in our hearts and on our minds. It was so honest.

What a beautiful and brave example my mom was to me in all of this. I will never ever forget how she, like the woman described in Proverbs 31, could even laugh at the days to come. My mom had an inner strength I aspire to.

2. Enjoy life right to the end

Jesus enjoyed life right to the end. Matthew 26:26 happens around a table, right before Jesus dies, and there He is eating and drinking with friends.

Mom loved being with her family and friends especially if it meant eating out at a great restaurant, having people in our home, or going on a great get away.... an adventure! Mom loved lively conversation, amusing stories, and coming along for the ride whatever the destination. Oh how I will miss saying to her,

"Hey mom, want to come grocery shopping with me?"

Simple things mom never said no to. She was always such terrific company.

In mom's "dying days" we squeezed some last things in:

- ☐ We went out to dinner together...one last time.
- ☐ Our girls, mom and I were able to go on one more adventure, to a local resort *(Sparkling Hills)*...one last time.
- ☐ When mom's brother and sisters came we were able to celebrate The Lord's Supper (Communion) around the table... one last time.
- ☐ I made some traditional dishes for her, even if she could only have one bite...one last time.
- ☐ We had a family picture taken...one last time.
- ☐ Mom made the effort to get to a Sunday church gathering...one last time.
- ☐ She always said "yes" to visits so she could see people...one last time

Another incredibly precious tradition was started when she learned she had a short time to live. We began a 10:00 p.m. meeting we called "Story Time." In 1989 mom began writing out stories of answered prayer – she kept 47 of them. Mom would read these stories to our family during her last days. Other friends and family would join in here and there and it became something absolutely unforgettable. We learned so many lessons through this and our love grew and grew.

One must live well to die well.

Incidentally, when we decided to publish these stories so that they would continue to be told, Mom thought it was pretty funny that, at 75, she was going to become an author.

That was mom, enjoying life right to the end.

3. It would be preferable to live than to die

Jesus didn't look forward to death and He prayed, asking if it might be avoided, even while wanting to be obedient to His calling.

Once, in the last week of mom's life, she suddenly said, "I don't want to go yet!" This came as a surprise because she was so looking forward to heaven.

As we thought about this we saw that while her communication was limited and her body was weak, she loved the intimacy of relationships from sisters and brothers, nieces and nephews, grandchildren, friends, and sons and daughters. I was her primary caregiver and we had a natural intimate role reversal and no wonder she didn't want to go!

I saw that, no matter how close people can be, there are still little rules relationships are governed by. As she walked through these dying days any last "walls" came down. Mom did not hold back any affection from me. She held my face and gazed into my eyes with such love it absolutely made me hold my breath. I felt as if she was studying me to remember every detail. I could see how she didn't want to let go of me.

One night as I tucked her into bed, she held her arms out to me three times and hugged me three times and, words limited at this point, she said with such feeling, "I love you, I love you, I love you <u>immensely</u>."

There are many, many good things about life and loving relationships and mom didn't simply "check out." She didn't have a fatalist attitude, or give up. Mom savored life and valued the time she had left in a healthy way and it was natural to think, "I don't want to let go just yet" because over a life-time she had developed wonderful friendships...they were hard to let go of, as it should be.

4. Forgive

Jesus forgave everyone, to the very end and even those mistreating Him when He died (Luke 23:34).

In Mom's stories you could see there were people who had made life challenging and there were people who had never made things right. Some things were still unresolved, but as she was dying she said, "In the end, what does it matter? It's not worth holding on to. We must forgive."

Mom demonstrated graciousness towards people in forgiveness and perspective. In her journal I found a list of people who had hurt or disappointed her; it wasn't a grudge list, it was a prayer list surrounded by Scriptures about grace and forgiveness. It is easy to forgive in the end if you have forgiven all the way along. She lived this out well.

This keeps speaking to me, this aspect of not clinging to grievances and not letting them steal joy. We must live our lives free from such hindrances, and act with generosity and forgiveness towards people.

5. Willing to die

It is hard to accept that a person actually has no options. In the beginning of all this, Mike was looking for other treatment options, other things to consider. Even when we knew the cancer was Stage 4, he was still brainstorming.

One day she looked at him and said with clarity and resolve, "You know Mike, God has extended my life longer than I was told I would live *(she had been told at one point she might not live past 40 due to a Kidney problem that troubled her earlier in her life)*. If God still has something for me to do, then God will heal me. If He says, 'That's good now,' then He will take me. So no, I won't be spending my days hunting for ways to survive. God is in control."

What a trust she had in God to be able to say this as Mom knew her life was in God's hands and she trusted Him with her death. She didn't get caught up in asking "why" over and over. She didn't go into "survival mode." She was going to die as she lived and with complete confidence that God's will would be done.

You have to think about this long before you get there and think about dying while you live so that you know what you know, what you know. Mom did this and it served her, and all of us, well.

* * *

As I watched my mom face her last days on earth I said to our kids, "We are being given a gift right now. We might not understand it all just yet, but one day we are going to come to look at death with far less fear than many. My mom has modeled for us what it looks like to be a follower of Christ in life, and now facing death with a sense of hope and courage. This will change you if you let it, and it will give you a strength you never knew you had."

Just before mom died she said something funny. She said, "How will I know when I am dead?"

I asked her what she meant and she said, "How will I know when I am dead? I have never done this before. Will someone tell me?"

I said, "You won't need anyone to tell you. Jesus will be there."

She said, "Yes Jesus will be there and He will say, 'Welcome here, Violet.'"

I said, "Yes, He will say, 'Welcome here, Violet. Well done.'"

Yes. Well done. For all I have received from my mother, and her example to me, I give thanks and say...well done.

"As the deer longs for streams of water,
so I long for you, O God.
I thirst for God, the living God.
When can I go and stand before Him?"

Psalm 42:1

CPSIA information can be obtained at www.ICGtesting.com
Printed in the USA
LVOW07s0802170316

479551LV00001B/32/P